Encouraged Growth:

A 40 Day Journey of

Encouragement and Prayers

D. R. KELLY

ISBN: 1542598133
ISBN-13: 978-1542598132

DEDICATION

This book is dedicated to everyone on every life journey. It is meant to remind you that you are not alone, and that you are loved more than you can possibly fathom. It is meant to embrace you, encourage you, challenge you, and to help you see beyond circumstances. This book was written in love, to help point you towards our greatest love, God. I pray your spirits are lifted, your faith is made stronger, and your journey be ever filled with the grace and peace of Jesus Christ. Know that you truly do matter.

Be blessed!

Dee

ACKNOWLEDGEMENT

I realized at a young age that I had something very rare and awesome in a mother. Cynthia Wade, the amount of love and support that God placed in you goes beyond anything I have been able to understand growing up. Where the trials of life chipped away at my outside, the Lord funneled His love through you to build and encourage me on a much needed deeper level. I love you more than anything I can express, and this book is a testament to God's great grace in my life, and your amazing influence as a mom to let me dream. Thank you for walking with me to see this one come true. I love you, Ma.

To the woman who a few us know dearly as, Auntie Elder Sister Barbara Jones. You have been a great friend on my journey with Christ for the last 11 years. In that time, you have been a constant and intricate part in my spiritual growth in ways that impact how I love and lead to this very day. I know that only God could bless us with such treasures in our lives, and for this I am grateful. The willingness and surrendered heart you have to God is a great example for all those that know you, and even though you did not want me to do this, I will risk receiving a loving scolding to simply say...thank you. You are the Paul to my Timothy. God bless you always.

Let's Begin!

DAY ONE

Be Encouraged! You have...

God-given Purpose

"So, my dear brothers and sisters, be strong and immovable. Always work enthusiastically for the Lord, for you know that nothing you do for the Lord is ever useless."

~1 Corinthians 15:58

God has given you purpose. Who you are and what you do matters. Who you are and what you do has great influence on those around you every day. Who you are and what you do will make a difference now, and for generations to come. Never discount how valuable you are. In all that you do, remember that God loves you so much, and your purpose and calling are an intricate part of His great and wonderful plan. Live in your truth...who you are and what you do matters.

Prayer:

Lord, please help me to remember that my life serves a greater purpose, which is Yours. Thank You for placing so much value in who I am as Your child, and entrusting me to serve You well in serving others. May the influence I pour into the lives of everyone I encounter reflect Your glorious and divine love always. In Jesus Christ's name I pray. Amen.

DAY TWO

Be Encouraged! You are...

God Approved

"For we are His workmanship [His own master work, a work of art], created in Christ Jesus [reborn from above--spiritually transformed, renewed, ready to be used] for good works, which God prepared [for us] beforehand [taking paths which He set], so that we would walk in them [living the good life which He prearranged and made ready for us]."

~Ephesians 2:10, AMP

People's opinion of you changes as easily as the direction of the wind. It is not consistent, and chasing these views for some sense of approval will leave you feeling tired, unsatisfied, and insecure. The GOOD NEWS is that we were not designed to live by the opinions of others. Our self-worth is rooted in the One who created us, made in His image, with purpose and extraordinary value. No matter what you face today and every day, it will never change how amazing you are and have been created to be. Remember, base your sense of value not on how others may "see" you, but on what GOD SAYS about you.

Prayer:

Father God, how amazing is Your hand that creates such beautifully unique treasures! Thank You for making me with so much love and great intention. Protect my thoughts from the lies that try to blind me to my truth which rests solely in You. Help me to remember that I am Your masterpiece, and that through Christ alone I am made worthy. In Jesus Christ's name I pray. Amen.

DAY THREE

Be Encouraged! You are...

Free Indeed

"So if the Son sets you free, you are truly free."
~ John 8:36

How often do we think about this truth? Through Christ, we have literally been set free. That means that we are not held by the condemnation and shame that the world tries to pressure us with. That means that you do not fall under any manipulating labels that Satan uses against you to steer you away from walking in your God-given truth. No, you have been set free by a loving Father, through His loving Son. Never forget that. Never forget your truth. Never forget who you are in Christ, and most importantly, NEVER forget just how much you are loved. Be blessed!

Prayer:

Thank You, God, for Jesus Christ and what He did on the cross for me. Thank You, Father, that I am no longer a slave to the things that seek to devour me. In You, Lord, I find my truth. In You, Lord, I find my freedom. In You, Lord, I am reminded that nothing and no one can ever change what You have done to redeem me and make me new. I am forever Yours. In Jesus Christ's name I glorify You. Amen!

DAY FOUR

Be Encouraged! Walk in...

God-fidence

"So do not throw away your confidence, which has a great reward. For you need endurance, so that after you have done God's will, you may receive what was promised."

~Hebrews 10:35-36, HCSB

Our confidence is best when it is rooted in things that are certain. Where the world tells us that we should grow in self-confidence, Scripture teaches us how to grow in God-confidence. One is temporary, deceiving, leads to becoming a hindrance in having a real relationship with God, and is fruitless in spiritual growth and maturation. The other is full of eternal love and promises, strength, and growth in love, joy, peace, patience, kindness, goodness, gentleness, faithfulness, and self-control (Gal. 5:22-23). It is good for us to know these differences, and it is even better to choose the one that gives us greater life. Be confident, but be confident in God above all things. Be blessed, Y'all!

Prayer:

My God, may I grow in confident trust in You and all that You are doing to raise me up in Your love. Help me to walk in Your patient endurance, discern the things that are of Your will, and be led by the eternal goodness of Your Holy Spirit. My life is in Your hands, most Sovereign and Faithful Father. In Jesus Christ's name I honor and praise You. Amen.

DAY FIVE

Be Encouraged! Stand strong in...

Steadfast God-fidence

"...Do not fear, for those who are with us are more than those who are with them."
~2 Kings 6:16, NKJV

In our walk with Christ we face many obstacles. By not conforming to the patterns of this world, we sometimes stick out and are subjected to judgment, ridicule, and persecution. Despite what we face in opposition, we need to remember to stand strong. Who we have faith in is bigger than all we encounter. Who we proclaim truth about is the One we receive true life from. Who we follow in love and humility is the One that grows us every step of the way in our walk. We must never throw this confidence in Him or His truth away. We remain God-confident because in Him is the true treasure of life everlasting. Be strong, love well, and find peace in His loving grace.

Prayer:

I praise You, Lord, that my strength is found in You. I give glory to You, God, for being the Rock and Protector of my soul. Though the world tries to tear me down, Your never-ending love always builds me up. I will not fear those who come against me because I follow You. Instead, I stand strong knowing that Your army surrounds me, and that I have already won the battle through Christ. Glory to God in the highest! In Christ's name I pray. Amen.

DAY SIX

Be Encouraged! Be bold in your...

Victorious Dependence

"You have also given me the shield of Your salvation, And Your right hand upholds and sustains me; Your gentleness [Your gracious response when I pray] makes me great."

~Psalms 18:35, AMP

It's so easy for us to think that we go through life on our own efforts. Satan loves for us to be so blinded. However, saved or unsaved, everyone is dependent on God and His sovereignty. Don't think so? Take a deep breath. That air you just took in? It is all Him. Those strong lungs you just used? Yes, all Him again. It is simple things like that in which we can really miss out on regarding the true blessing of a supportive and helpful Father. He has given us His shield of victory through Jesus Christ. We have been set apart, yet we are never alone. God is constant in our lives at every moment, and He desires to see us grow. Your life journey is one of greatness. Don't diminish what God has begun in you. Embrace it...and while you're at it, embrace Him even more.

Prayer:

Thank You, Father God, that Your heavenly design never included us doing life without You. You are there in every thought and at every moment. I can never thank You enough for the support and victory through every trial and triumph. My only hope is that my life reflects Your holy love, and never stops in bringing glory to Your majesty. May You forever reign in my life. In Jesus Christ's mighty name I pray. Amen!

DAY SEVEN

Be Encouraged! You radiate in...

Holy Couture

"Since God chose you to be the holy people he loves, you must clothe yourselves with tenderhearted mercy, kindness, humility, gentleness, and patience."

~Colossians 3:12

It can be so easy to exist in our day-to-day lives with a skewed perception of others. Life through Christ, however, offers us so much greater. Through the shedding of our old selves, we are now clothed in God's goodness and filled with His Holy Spirit. Walk in this truth with the love and humility that shouts of the glory of God. You look good in them God genes, wear them well. Be blessed!

Prayer:

Most Holy and Loving Father, thank You, that You have called me by name to be one of Your children. Thank You, that I am forever a part of Your glorious family and kingdom. Thank You, that I no longer wear the death that sin brought me, but now I am clothed in Your goodness and righteousness. Through Your Holy Spirit I am set apart, and Your magnificent light shines through my every fiber. I surrender myself as a fragrant offering to glorify You through the gift of true life received through Your Son, My Lord and Savior, Jesus Christ. In His mighty name I give You all praise and honor. Amen!

DAY EIGHT

Be Encouraged! Be consumed with...

Perfect Peace

"You will keep the mind that is dependent on You in perfect peace, for it is trusting in You."
~Isaiah 26:3, HCSB

In this day and age, it is easy to get caught up in the hustle and bustle of everyday life. Stress sometimes feels like it goes hand in hand with all of that, but when we read God's truth we see hope for better. This verse reminds us that if we trust in and keep our thoughts fixed on Him, He will give us perfect peace. I don't know about you, but I certainly would love to live in that gift every day. I pray that as you read this you have that perfect peace of God in every moment of every day.

Prayer:

Abba, Great and Glorious Father, Most Holy of Holies, You are every good and great thing that I experience in my life. Thank You, that although I face all kinds of trials and obstacles, I can come to You freely knowing that You will fill me with Your perfect peace. Thank You that I do not have to be consumed with the struggles that vie for my thoughts, but that through Your Holy Spirit Your peace is poured abundantly in every ounce *of me. Help me to always look to You. May I remain in a constant and whole-hearted surrender to You. May all my thoughts forever be obedient unto Jesus Christ, and I grow closer to You with this gift of life and love You have given me. In Jesus Christ's wonderful name I pray, Amen.*

DAY NINE

Be Encouraged! You are the image of...

God's Great Love

"We all, with unveiled faces, are looking as in a mirror at the glory of the Lord and are being transformed into the same image from glory to glory; this is from the Lord who is the Spirit."

~2 Corinthians 3:18, HCSB

True love comes from the Father because He is love. As God's children we really do have EVERY opportunity to show the love we receive freely to others. This is especially important in these days where loveless acts seem to be shamelessly glorified through social media, television, and/or news. Let's make an effort as God's kids to let the love of Christ shine through like the radiant sun in how we live out our faith. Love is stronger than everything and it ALWAYS wins. Live, love, serve.

Prayer:

What an amazing thing to be created by love, in love, and for love! Thank You, Lord, for creating me with such great purpose. May I never lose sight of my calling to reflect Your beautiful and redeeming love in these days where the challenge and opposition against You is so much. Help me continue to stand strong and love stronger. May the influence I have on others radiate of Your goodness and my faith in You. Let me draw nearer to You, and may Your Holy Spirit continue to grow me more and more like our Everlasting King and Savior, Jesus Christ! In His name I pray. Amen.

DAY TEN

Be Encouraged! You were created to ...

Imitate Love

"Therefore be imitators of God as dear children. And walk in love, as Christ also loved us and given Himself for us, an offering and a sacrifice to God for a sweet-smelling aroma."

~Ephesians 5:1-2, NKJV

The life we choose to live is always representative of what we believe is at our core. Our true identity is more than a latest fad, struggles we go through, or ambitious gain. It is what drives us in how we think, act, and speak. As Christians our identity is found solely in the Father. It is important to know this, so that we follow and imitate Jesus Christ Who is our perfect example of living as what we are created to be...love. Remember, we were created by Love, to be loved, and BE love. Do it well!

Prayer:

Father God, we know that children often resemble their parents. Not just physically, but behaviorally as well. I count it joy that I have been created in the image of my heavenly PaPa, and am called to imitate all that He has taught me through my Savior, Friend, and Co-Heir to His kingdom, Jesus Christ. Although the world tries to distract me from knowing who and Whose I am, You never cease in drawing me near to remind me of my truth. At Your feet I sit, and I give myself to Your will and beautiful purpose. I love You. In Jesus Christ's name I pray. Amen.

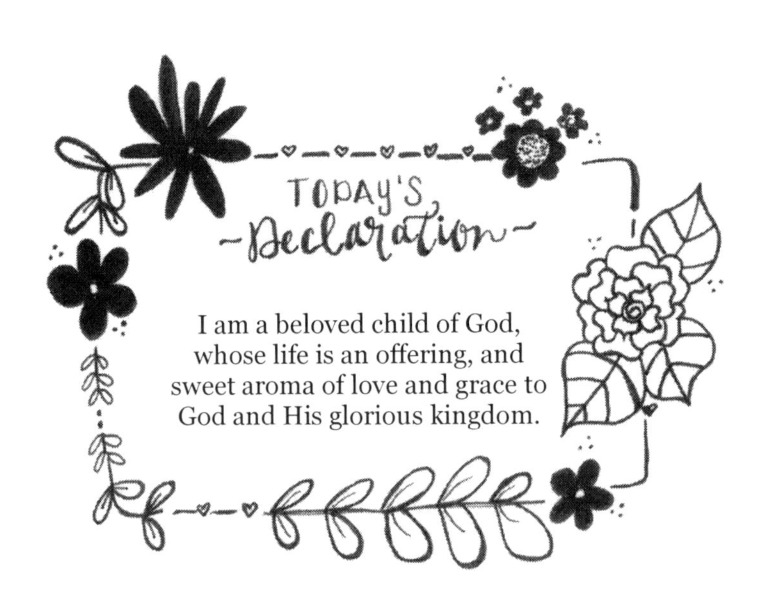

DAY ELEVEN

Be Encouraged! You are protected by...

All Encompassing Love

"Finally, be strong in the Lord and in the strength of His might. Put on the full armor of God, so that you will be able to stand firm against the schemes of the devil."

~ Ephesians 6:10-11, NASB

It is SO important that we be renewed in our minds. The more our minds are filled with the truth of God's Word, the less susceptible we are to Satan's deceptions and temptations. For anyone going through rough times just know that God sees, and more importantly, He cares. He wants to see you through this time because He LOVES you. You were His before you were placed in this world. He wants to see you to be healed, He wants to see you restored, and He wants to see you filled with His joy. He wants you to draw closer to Him so He can bless your life with more than all you ever imagine or ask for. Let Him do so, call on Him. He promised that He will answer.

Prayer:

Thank You, Lord, for the comfort of Your open arms. Through every trial and tribulation I may face, You remind me that I can come to the altar and receive unending love. Take all my burdens, God, as I lay them down before You. Restore me in the deepest areas that only You can reach. Renew my heart and mind with the peace and healing of a heavenly Father that will do anything to protect me as His treasured child. May I always rejoice in the all encompassing love and care of Your goodness and grace, Lord. In Jesus Christ's name, I trust You. Amen.

DAY TWELVE

Be Encouraged! Remember to...

Breathe In, Pray Out

"Are any of you suffering hardships? You should pray. Are any of you happy? You should sing praises. Are any of you sick? You should call for the elders of the church to come and pray over you, anointing you with oil in the name of the Lord."

~James 5:13-14

Prayer is SO important. Just as our body needs oxygen to breathe, our spirit needs God to breathe. C. S. Lewis wrote, "I pray because I cannot help myself. I pray because I'm helpless. I pray because the need flows out of me all the time - waking and sleeping. It doesn't change God - it changes me." It is in Lewis' candid confession that we see a resounding truth for all of us. We just simply cannot function at our best without communicating with God. While there is no set way to talk to the Father, we do have to come with our whole heart...regardless of its condition. He ALWAYS takes us "as is". We all have issues. Let us start and/or keep talking to our Father about them.

Prayer:

Lord, may I always remember that I can come boldly before You with all of my prayers and petitions. May I trust and believe that even when I struggle with this, Your Holy Spirit goes before You on my behalf with utterances that only You understand. How awesome is it that I don't have to be anything but me when I come before You! How even more awesome are Your affections for me in always listening and answering! Thank You, Lord, for Your gentle ear, comforting arms, and never-ending love for me. I love You. In Jesus Christ's name I pray. Amen.

DAY THIRTEEN

Be Encouraged! Stand firm in your...

Seeds of Truth

"Now if any of you lacks wisdom, he should ask God, who gives to all generously without criticizing, and it will be given to him. But let him ask in faith without doubting. For the doubter is like the surging sea, driven and tossed by the wind."

~James 1:5-6, HCSB

Self-doubt is such a destructive spirit in our lives. It is rooted in fear, and definitely not something God designed for us to operate in. Satan knows this, and he will jump at any chance he can to lead us astray on a wave of emotional self-doubt. We have to learn to be alert to the seeds of lies and deception that the enemy tries to deposit in our thoughts. The more we are in tune with God's truth, the less static we hear from an accuser that truly has no power over our lives. We get to choose what voice we listen to. Let today be the day that you choose to listen only to what is edifying to your spirit. Let today be the day that you stand firm in your truth that rests solely in your loving Creator and Father in heaven. As you read this, may you be filled with all the goodness, kindness, and grace of God. May you find that your footsteps spring with joy and your air smell of a fragrant and holy treasure. Remember that you are a gem, and no lie will ever change your truth. Be blessed!

Prayer:

Thank You, Father God, that Your truth opens my eyes to who I really am in You. Though the enemy seeks to destroy me, through Christ he is rendered powerless over me as Your beloved. May the only seeds that take root in my spirit be from You alone. Lord, sift out any weeds of self-doubt that seek to choke out Your truth. May I walk like I truly know Whose I am and who I am. I surrender my thoughts to You so they may be obedient unto Christ. May Your thoughts and Your ways forever reign over my life in every step of my journey. In Jesus Christ's name I pray. Amen.

DAY FOURTEEN

Be Encouraged! As God's child, you are...

Always Connected

"Neither death nor life, neither angels nor demons, neither our fears for today nor our worries about tomorrow-not even the powers of hell can separate us from God's love."

~Romans 8:38b

We cannot allow negative thoughts to convince us that we are not in alignment with God because we are. Once we accept Christ as our Lord and Savior, we are in alignment with the Father. We may need to focus more on Him, but we are still very much in alignment because of what Christ did on the cross in bridging the gap between us and the Father. Perspective is everything.

Prayer:

Lord, the lies of this world try to convince me that there are moments where I am not connected to You. However, Your word tells me that there is nothing that can ever get in between what I have with You through Your Son and my Savior, Jesus Christ. Thank You that I do not have to fear going through my life journey without You. Thank You that You are the whisper and wind that directs my paths. Help me to never lose sight of this, and may I never lose faith in You as my omnipresent Father. I will cling to You all the days of my life, and forever more. In Jesus Christ's name. Amen.

DAY FIFTEEN

Be Encouraged! Be led with...

Right Thinking

"The righteous person faces many troubles, but the LORD comes to the rescue each time."

~Psalms 34:19

We all have moments in life which bring trials and difficulties. God tells us this in the verse above. However, He also says that He will deliver us through all of those things. When we face adversity we have a choice to believe His truth, or believe the lies of Satan. One side promises peace, deliverance, healing, forgiveness, restoration, love, and other things that promote spiritual growth. The other side only seeks to steal, kill, and destroy who we are and what we are created to be. We have a choice as to what we believe. It is as simple as life or death...because that's what it really is.

Prayer:

Lord, today and every day moving forward I choose to believe Your wonderful truth. Though I may face many difficulties in my life journey, I know that I am not alone because You are with me. Your loving hand provides a way for me to go through every struggle, and Your promises of mercy and deliverance line the path of every step I take. May my thoughts always be consumed with the truth that Your love for me never fails no matter the season I am in. Nothing is greater than You and the love You have for me. I am found, I am Yours, I have life, and I am blessed. In Jesus Christ's name I pray. Amen.

DAY SIXTEEN

Be Encouraged! Remember that...

Perspective Matters

"And now dear brothers and sisters, one final thing. Fix your thoughts on what is true, and honorable, and right, and pure, and lovely, and admirable. Think about things that are excellent and worthy of praise."
~Philippians 4:8

When we talk about being flawed as a "human condition", what perspective do we have? Is it one of condemnation, where we focus more on the fact that as people we are prone to screw up? Do we see our mistakes and sin as a definitive part of our makeup and identity? Or do we have the perspective that focuses more on the grace and glory of a perfect God, Who in loving mercy saved us from the wages of sin? Do we see that we have been made new, the old is gone, and a perfect God dwells within us? Where our identity, and who we are, no longer rests in our flaws and sins, but in a Father, Savior, and Comforter that grows us in our weaknesses. Where we recognize that our strength is not our own, but of a great and sovereign King that claims us as His own, and will never let anything or anyone separate us from Him.

See, PERSPECTIVE MATTERS. What lens you use to see your humanness matters. You get to pick and choose: a conditioned worldly lens, or a redeemed godly lens. Be encouraged today though. As a believer, you are God's own, and who you are rests in Jesus Christ. I don't have to know you to know that you are beautiful, you absolutely are. So instead of seeing your flaws and sin as a part of your condition and identity, see it as an opportunity for the love and strength of God in you to be glorified as He spiritually grows you in His perfection. Be blessed!

Prayer:

Heavenly Father, thank You for Jesus Christ, and that through Him I am no longer a slave to sin. Through Christ's sacrifice on the cross for Your created, I am chosen, I am forgiven, I am redeemed, I am righteous, I am free, I am saved, I am made new, I am loved, I am a child of the Most High. I am Yours, Lord. May the lens I choose to use always be the one that You have given me. May I rejoice in my true identity which is made in the image of Your gloriousness. Thank You for Your perfect love which casts out all things that try to go against Your truth in and for me. I glorify and honor You always. In Jesus Christ's name I pray. Amen!

DAY SEVENTEEN

Be Encouraged! Be consumed with...

Loving Thoughts

"Set your mind on the things that above, not on the things that are on earth."

~Colossians 3:2, NASB

Our thoughts have a heavy impact on what we say and do. Being made new in Christ Jesus means that instead of thinking on the stressful things in this hurt-filled world, we can think on God's response to all of...which begins with love. WWJD (What Would Jesus Do) isn't some catchy phrase; it literally is how we should think on EVERYTHING. In whatever you are facing today, find peace as you think on things of heaven, not things on earth. Hugs.

Prayer:

God, there are so many things that fight for me to be moved by my emotions. Issues in society, relationships with family and friends, and even my own inner battles in recognizing and holding to who I am in Christ. I pray that You would consume my thoughts, Lord. Take from me any thought that goes against Your goodness, Your will, and Your love for me. Help me to see as You see more and more each day. May I rest in Your peace so that my mind, body, and soul respond to the experiences I face in my life journey in a way that reflects upward thinking. I love You, Lord. In Jesus Christ's name I pray. Amen.

DAY EIGHTEEN

Be Encouraged! Grow with God in...

Unshakeable Faith

"He did not waver in unbelief at God's promise but was strengthened in his faith and gave glory to God, because he was fully convinced that what He promised He was also able to perform."

~Romans 4:20-21, HCSB

In Romans chapter 4, Paul gives us an example of the unwavering faith we should have in God. Abraham believed God in a way that left no room for doubt in what he trusted God to do. It is not a far stretch for us to live like this, too. It begins by actively being in relationship with our Father through Jesus Christ, and knowing that He absolutely loves you. You matter to God. Let Him love you into stronger faith. Be blessed!

Prayer:

Lord, may I grow in the same grace that Abraham received from You. May I grow in Your strength to where I no longer consider the lies that Satan tries to destroy me with. May the words of my mouth, mediations of my heart, and fruit that I bear reveal a faith that does not waver in the face of my adversary and tribulations living in a fallen and hurt world. Father God, may I always remember Your great love for me before all else. In the precious and glorious name of my Savior, Jesus Christ, I pray. Amen!

DAY NINETEEN

Be Encouraged! You are the...

Master's Builder

"Do not withhold good from those who deserve it when it is in your power to help them."
~Proverbs 3:27

The two greatest commandments that God has given us are to love Him, and love others. As the Father fills us and grows us in spiritual maturity, we are to share it with those we have relationships with. In Christ-like humility, we look to the interest of others by building them up in godly truth, encouragement, and love. We never pass up moments to do the good we are called to as God's created for God's created. Let's serve well, and remember that it is all for His kingdom.

Prayer:

Thank You, Father God, for sending Your Son, Jesus Christ. Thank You, that through my great and mighty Savior I have love and life; and that I get to share it with others. Thank You that I have Your Holy Spirit to guide, teach, and grow me in the ways of being made in Your image. In a world that craves relationship, acceptance, and love, it is through Your holy power that You fill me and send me out to steward well in Christ-like humility. May I continue to serve and honor You by building others up in Your love and truth for them. May I never take this responsibility lightly. May I always have godly truth on my tongue, and Your love in my heart with everyone I meet in my journey. In Jesus Christ's name I pray. Amen.

DAY TWENTY

Be Encouraged! Taste God's...

Soul Food

"Don't be impressed with your own wisdom. Instead, fear the Lord and turn away from evil. Then you will have healing for your body and strength for your bones."

~Proverbs 3:7-8

Human reasoning is extremely deceptive. We can convince ourselves that we actually know better than God does in our life's journey. The more we know, the less we need Him; and the less we need Him, the more vulnerable we are to destructive living. However, if we turn from ourselves to the Father, then the promises that come with reverent fear of the Lord will produce spiritual health that overflows into our physical, mental, and emotional well-being. God is always going to be our greatest Doctor. Developing a healthy relationship with the Lord will always lead to a healthy soul. Live well.

Prayer:

Lord, I surrender my all unto You. Fill me with Your wisdom and with Your blessings, Father God. May I not be led astray by my flesh, or the things of this world as I live my life committed to You. May I grow in Your ever-loving and all-knowing grace. May I be the kind of child that is humble, yet bold in living a life that is pleasing and fragrant to You and You alone. I pray I never get to a point in my journey where I do not need or desire to seek You, Lord. Thank You for being at the core of who I am, and what I am created to be. May my soul forever be nourished by Your great and awesome majesty. All praises I sing unto You, in Jesus Christ's name. Amen!

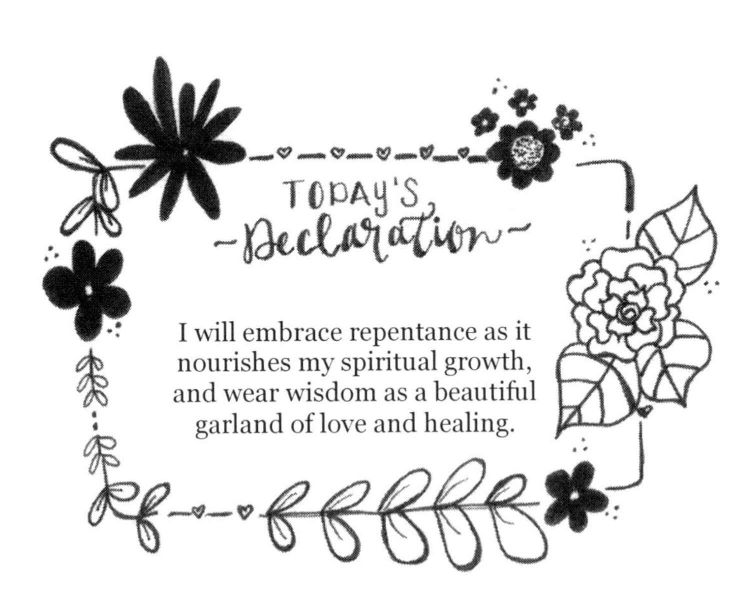

DAY TWENTY-ONE

Be Encouraged! Be led by...

True Love

"Do not take revenge or bear a grudge against members of your community, but love your neighbor as yourself; I am Yahweh."
~Leviticus 19:18, HCSB

It took some time for me to understand early in my walk what God meant by this command. There is a BIG difference between God's love and the world's version of it. Love really is powerful in how it is unashamed, unconditional, and edifying to its core. To truly give love, we have to know Who it comes from, how we were created in it, how we receive it daily, and how we are to recognize ourselves as being it so that we can see it in others. It is rather simple; God is love, and we are created in His image. How can we not view each other in the same truth? Blessings!

Prayer:

Heavenly Father, may I lean in and receive wisdom from You. May I walk with You, and learn to discern Your love from all else that is not real. Bless me to never grow weary, disheartened, or emotionally led in how I love others in my life journey. Help me to see them through Your lens, and to love them through Your will and truth. May my godly loving of another never be dependent on them or their response, but may it be solely dependent on You and how You have called me to live. May I never forget that I am an ambassador of Christ and Your great love for us as I serve others. Consume me, Holy Spirit. Consume my heart, and lead me in the way I should walk. In Jesus Christ's name. Amen.

DAY TWENTY-TWO

Be Encouraged! Find peace through...

Necessary Forgiveness

"For everyone has sinned; we all fall short of God's glorious standard. Yet God freely and graciously declares that we are righteous."

~Romans 3:23-24

Forgiveness can be a tough command to follow. We do not like being wrong, and we despise being hurt. So we get led by our emotions and may be driven by bitterness, anger, and/or resentment. As God's kids, we are called to live contrary to this. We are called to forgive everyone everything because that is what Christ did for us. Even unto His last breath on the cross, He prayed for our forgiveness. The question we should ask ourselves when we struggle with forgiving anyone, including ourselves, is this: "If Jesus, being the One who created us all, forgave us, then how can *we* not be forgiving?" We literally have no place to hold things against anybody else, and by doing so means that we feel we are in a higher regard or authority over Christ. Yes, forgiveness frees the other person. Yes, in forgiving we find peace. However, the bigger reason is that we forgive because God forgave.

Prayer:

Jesus, I thank You for seeing me beyond my transgressions and human condition in this fallen world. You see me as the child You fearfully and wonderfully made before I was even formed in my mother's womb. It is through this love that You have also forgiven me. Freed me. Given me life. It is through this great act of love and forgiveness that I am no longer separated from my Father. May I never forget the great sacrifice You made for me, even in the midst of my sin. May I remember what You have done in love, so that I can in the same Christ-like humility offer it to others. May my heart never hold grudges, anger, bitterness, resentment, or any other soul destructive emotion against any person, or situation. Help me to see and lead in love always, especially when my flesh tries to convince me to do otherwise. May You reign in how I love. In Your glorious name I pray. Amen.

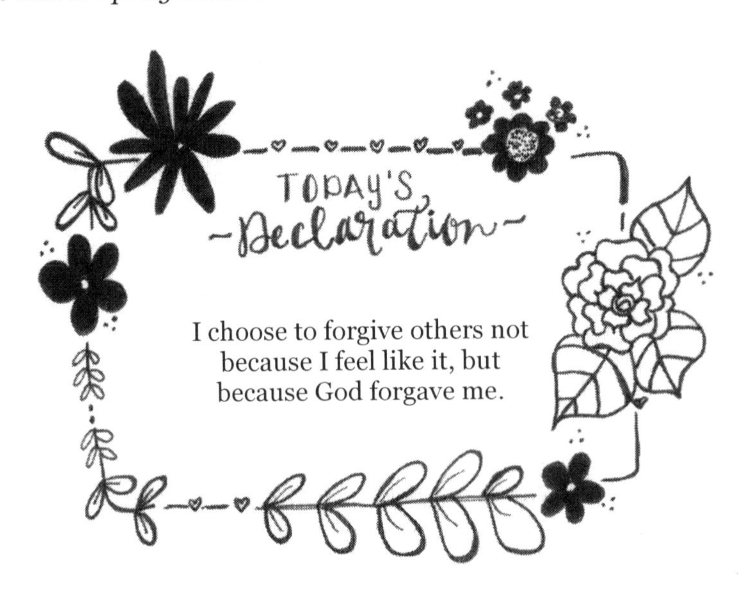

DAY TWENTY-THREE

Be Encouraged! You can choose to...

Flee from Sin

"Make allowance for each other's faults, and forgive anyone who offends you. Remember, the Lord forgave you, so you must forgive others."
~Colossians 3:13

We all sin. The choice that was made in the Garden of Eden set the way for us to be born sinful into a sinful world. As much as we would like to give Eve the side eye for eating the fruit from the tree, the truth is that we still make choices that go against God's will for us. No sin is greater than another because God still sees it all the same. It is unfortunate that the world conditions us to categorize sin on levels. We make the mistake of believing this makes sense so we can feel justified in our reaction to sin. However, nothing justifies wrong behavior, and when we are not mindful as God instructs, we can fall into the same trap of committing sin (Galatians 6:1-2). We have to stop acting like God is okay with us going against Him. If He was, we would not need Jesus, and we would not need to repent. Sin happens, but it is what we do to change from it that matters most. No one is exempt from this truth.

Prayer:
Holy Spirit, it is through Your power that I receive the gifts of Your fruit which produce life. Through Your wisdom and teaching I learn how to walk in joy, peace, patience, kindness, goodness, faithfulness, gentleness, and self-control. Help me to grow stronger in living out these acts of love with all those I encounter. Help me to always show love, especially through the act of forgiveness. May I be quick to forgive and even quicker to take every opportunity You bless me with to build someone up. Help me to see people through Your eyes, and not the pain of living in a fallen world. Hurting people, hurt people; but Your loving children love. May Your truth guide my heart and actions. In Jesus Christ's name I pray. Amen.

DAY TWENTY-FOUR

Be Encouraged! Through Christ there is...

Freedom in Forgiveness

"But God demonstrates His own love toward us, in that while we were still sinners, Christ died for us."
~Romans 5:8, NKJV

Forgiveness is one of the hardest acts of love for us to show towards one another. It goes against the very nature of our flesh, which is easily offended and emotionally driven. When we are wronged, our natural tendency is to do wrong back. However, Jesus teaches us not to pay back an eye for an eye, but rather to love. Love covers a multitude of sins (1 Peter 4:8). Our greatest example of this is Christ dying on the cross for us for the forgiveness of all our sins. He forgave us, with no strings attached. He forgave us, even in the midst of us turning on Him. He forgave us because He loves us. Who do you need to set free through forgiveness from the prison of your hurt? Who do you need to show love to in the way Christ shows love for you every day? It may be difficult to do, but the spiritual freedom found in being obedient to this command is well worth the emotional sacrifice. Be strong in God's love, and know that I am rooting for you.

Prayer:

How great is the love You have for me, Jesus! Forgive me, Lord, for not always walking in the freedom You sacrificed on the cross for me so long ago. Forgive me for being led by emotions, instead of being led by Your Holy Spirit, the gift and Wonderful Counselor You sealed me with for eternity. I pray, Holy Spirit, that You would convict my heart and open my eyes to see who I need to set free from the bondage of my hurt. May I be wary in holding anything over another, except love. Help me, Lord, to see and discern people apart from the things they do. May I respond to hurt, offense, opposition, and trials in a way that is pleasing to You, and beneficial to my soul. Be my strength when this is difficult, and help me remember that through Your love we all receive the same freedom in forgiveness. May my heart be led in this truth above all else. In Jesus Christ's name I pray. Amen.

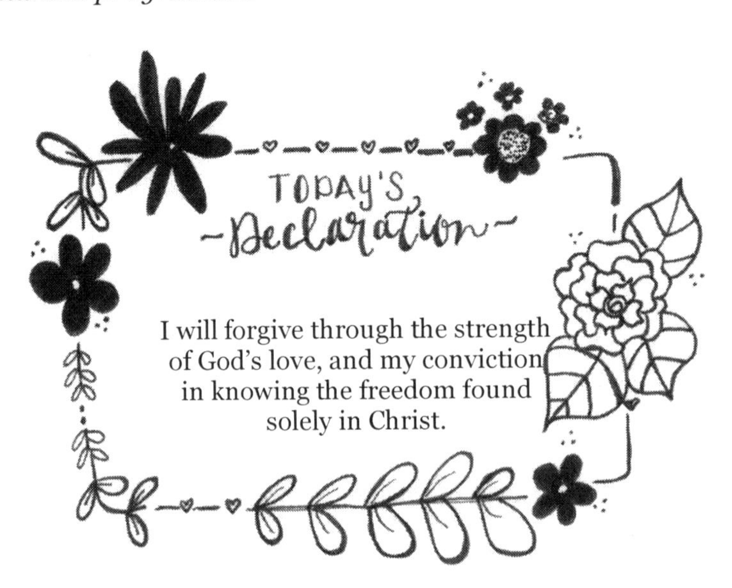

DAY TWENTY-FIVE

Be Encouraged! You are called and...

Seasoned by the Spirit

"Conduct yourselves with wisdom towards outsiders, making the most of the opportunity. Let your speech always be with grace, as though seasoned with salt, so that you will know how you should respond to each person."

~Colossians 4:5-6, NASB

God desires for those whom He has called to love Him, and to love others as He has shown through Jesus Christ. We are to be the salt of the earth; seasoned in His Word, and preserving this spiritual food through all we say, do, and think. Every day we should strive to live as an offering to God that is salted with fire. Every day we should acknowledge and act on the opportunity to edify His kingdom. Think about how salty you are in your walk with Christ. How can YOU season others in your day today? You are a blessing!

Prayer:

How I long to be pleasing in Your sight, Lord! It is through Your Holy Spirit that I am called to walk in the fruit that is edifying to my soul. It is through Your same Holy Spirit that I am called to pour these edifying seeds of life and love into every beautiful person I encounter. Even though Your children are all in so many different places in our life journeys, we are on the same path to seeking and being in relationship with You. May I never grow stale in my pursuit of You. May I always remain seasoned and ready to be used by Your Holy Spirit. May I walk bold in Your truth, and share freely in Your love. May my spirit be stirred for You, my steps be firm, my tongue saturated in encouragement, my mind focused on things above, and my heart girded with Your wisdom and love. In Jesus Christ's name. Amen!

DAY TWENTY-SIX

Be Encouraged! Be grown in…

Holy Perfection

"And we have come to know and to believe the love God has for us. God is love, and the one who remains in love remains in God, and God remains in him. In this, love is perfected with us so that we may have confidence in the day of judgment..."

~1 John 4:16-17, HCSB

Perspective is everything. We constantly run around saying that we are not perfect, but what does that mean? As a believer, we have perfection in us through Christ. Although, we alone are not perfect, we have a perfect Christ within us. This means that as we live daily, we strive to grow *in* His perfection to maturity that is pleasing to the Father. It goes with gaining an understanding of who we are, Whose we are, and Who He is within us.

Prayer:

Lord, help me to walk with clarity and truth in understanding what true perfection is. Though the world tries to convince me that I can gain this by my own efforts, Your love reminds me that the perfection within me is of Jesus. Through the indwelling of Your Holy Spirit, each day I walk with You is a day that Your unfailing love grows and perfects me. Thank You that I do not have the burden of trying to be anything but what You created and called me to be. May my eyes always be lifted to You, my heart be open to receive You, and my walk be committed to following You all the days of my life. Oh praise the One who gave it all, and loves me eternally. In Jesus Christ's name I pray. Amen!

DAY TWENTY-SEVEN

Be Encouraged! You have been...

Filled by the Holy Spirit

"But the Holy Spirit produces this kind of fruit in our lives: love, joy, peace, patience, kindness, goodness, faithfulness, gentleness, self-control..."

~Galatians 5:22-23a

How often do we find ourselves praying for peace, joy, patience, etc.? As Christ followers we have these characteristics in us already through the Holy Spirit. We just simply need to walk in them. Our prayers reflect what we believe and understand in our relationship with the Father. Walk in His truth today, and when it is difficult, remember to ask the Holy Spirit to help you exercise the fruit you have been filled with. Love and hugs!

Prayer:

El Shaddai, Most Holy God, the One who loves me eternally, may the words of my mouth and the meditations of my heart be forever pleasing in Your sight. May I live life in a way that reflects my belief and great love for You. May I never lose sight of Your Holy Spirit Who walks with me in every moment, and fills me with everything I need to get through all my days. Life may throw curve balls, but Your grace and mercy makes all my crooked paths straight. Help me, Lord, to continue growing strong in the gifts You have given me to stand strong and endure in the face of every moment, whether difficult or not. Thank You, Lord, for being all I need. In Jesus Christ's name I pray. Amen.

DAY TWENTY-EIGHT

Be Encouraged! Love is the value of...

Relational Fees

"Don't be selfish; don't try to impress others. Be humble, thinking of others as better than yourselves. Don't look out for your own interests, but take an interest in others, too."

~Philippians 2:3-4

It is so beneficial to healthy relationships when we are *intentional with our intention* towards others. Paying attention may seem simple enough, but there are times when we are just "waiting for our turn". Philippians 2:1-11 teaches about the humility of Christ, and what it looks like to be attentive while looking to the interest of others. Be encouraged today as you work towards being more present with those you interact with. Not only will you let them know that they truly do matter, but you will be nurturing a necessary part of building a healthy God-designed relationship. Remember, "Paying attention is the currency of healthy relationships" (Kevin Queen). You only get today once, so make sure to see and share the joy in it. Now go, and walk in that love. Blessings!

Prayer:

Father God, thank You for showing me through Christ how to be in holy relationships. In a world that tells me that relationships are give and take, You teach me that I am called to give. I am called to give my time, attention, and love. I am to give to others in a way that builds them up, and let them know that they matter. This is the kind of love that we truly long for in this hurting world. As You continue to fill me, may I never grow weary in pouring it out into every one You bring before me. All for Your glory and kingdom, In Jesus Christ's name. Amen!

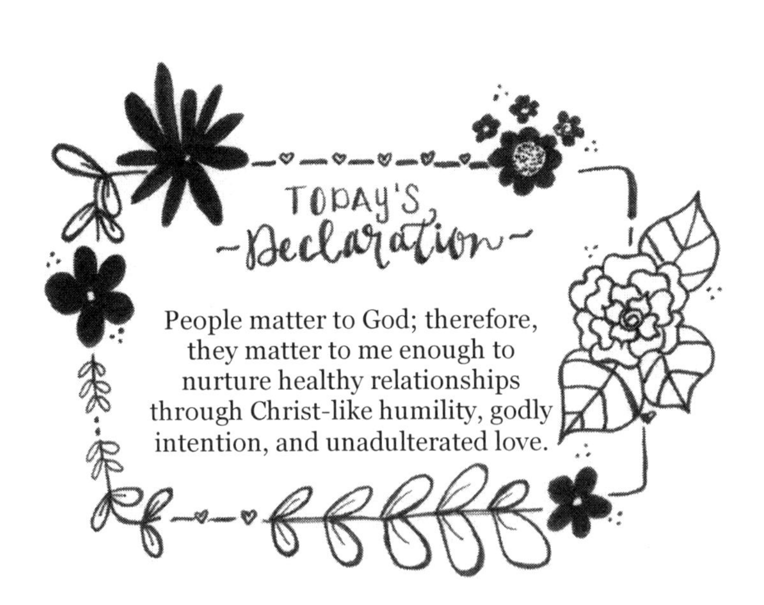

DAY TWENTY-NINE

Be Encouraged! Receive God's...

True Treasure

"Don't copy the behavior and customs of this world, but let God transform you into a new person by changing the way you think. Then you will learn to know God's will for you, which is good and pleasing and perfect." ~Romans 12:2

The things we should truly value in this world are our relationship with God, and the understanding we gain from Him. Worldly success is fleeting, and does not last any longer than the time it was given to shine by the One who created it. We get so caught up in the things of this world which we believe validates who we are. So we do and say things to generate the greatest applause. The problem is that regardless of how resounding the world's cheer of acceptance is, it will never fill what we need to be satisfied. It was never meant to.

The significance we seek can only be found in the One who made us, the One whom we were made in the image of, the One who is at the core of all He has created...God. No amount of money can buy what Jesus Christ paid in full for us on the cross. Redemption is a gift that we receive freely when we let go of the things that lead us to death. We cannot take worldly treasures with into eternity, but we can LIVE in eternity with our true treasure, which is Christ.

Prayer:

Lord, forgive me for ever seeking the approval of man above You. Sometimes I forget that I already have been accepted and approved by You through Christ. May I grow stronger in the truth You have spoken over my life. May I focus more on You, and less on the things of this world. May I grow in understanding my worth found solely in Christ. May I walk in the redemption I have received from You, and no longer chase the wind of worldly things that can never satisfy my soul the way You do. Thank You that my true treasure rests in You, and that I get to spend eternity with You. With You my heart is full, and I rejoice in Your goodness and mercy. In Jesus Christ's wonderful name I pray. Amen!

DAY THIRTY

Be Encouraged! Hear the sound of Jesus...

Calling All Messengers

"Also I heard the voice of the Lord saying: "Whom shall I send, And who will go for Us?" Then I said, "Here I am! Send me.""
~Isaiah 6:8, NKJV

As Christ followers, our lives should reflect God's love. The Gospel of Christ is truth that breathes life into the very essence of who we are, and how we live. We are ambassadors; messengers of God's great love for us, and what He has done for us all through Jesus Christ. We are forgiven, we have been made righteous, we are clean...we are free. Free in and through the love of a Father Who loves us beyond our circumstances. This is the message we live out. This is the message we share. Go share it. Love and hugs, Y'all.

Prayer:
As Your child, God, I call You Yahweh Shammah for You are my Lord who is always there. You have called me to be Yours, and have drawn me nearer to You. I pray that I always respond to the calling You have for me with a resounding, "Here I am! Send me!" May I go with Your full armor, and a boldness that is Holy Spirit led. May Your breath that fills my soul be the wind of glory that directs my everything. I am Your vessel, Lord, and it is a pure blessing and honor that I am a steward for Your great majesty. May I serve well with surrendered heart, and unwavering faith. In Christ's name I pray always. Amen.

DAY THIRTY-ONE

Be Encouraged! Let your tongue be sweet with...

Gentle Speech

"A servant of the Lord must not quarrel but must be kind to everyone, be able to teach, and be patient with difficult people. Gently instruct those who oppose the truth. Perhaps God will change those people's hearts, and they will learn the truth."

~2 Timothy 2:24-25

As a child of God, know this: opposition will come. It is important to remember that we live in a fallen and hurt-filled world. This means that every single person we encounter, saved and unsaved, has a different view point from the one we have. Even though we truly believe that we understand this simple truth, we do not always respond to these differences so well. Not seeing "eye-to-eye" with someone else can sometimes be quite a struggle. However, if we choose in our walk with Christ to be more Holy Spirit led, then we will be less emotionally led. All it takes is to breathe, listen to the Holy Spirit's guidance, and with love speak only what is beneficial and wise. Remember, it is always better to be righteous than to be "right". You can do it!

Prayer:

Lord, I confess that I have not always met difference and opposition in a way that is pleasing to You. Forgive me for giving in to my emotions, instead of holding on to Your grace and guidance. From this day forward, may the words I use be kind, teachable, filled with patience, and grounded in Your truth. Help me to rest in the understanding that true change within any of us occurs through Your Holy Spirit, and that I am a vessel of Your love. May I pour into others only what You have been pouring into me. I surrender my all to Your guidance and discernment, and I thank You for blessing me with such a great honor in building up and encouraging my brothers and sisters in Your kingdom. For Your glory! In Jesus Christ's name. Amen!

DAY THIRTY-TWO

Be Encouraged! You can endure with...

God's Faithful Gifts

"No temptation has overtaken you except what is common to humanity. God is faithful, and He will not allow you to be tempted beyond what you are able, but with temptation He will also provide a way of escape so that you are able to bear it."

~1 Corinthians 10:13, HCSB

This world is a melting pot of distractions and enticements. It can be difficult at times to process through all the desires and temptations we face daily. Big or small, we all struggle to determine what is beneficial versus what is permissible. Can you relate to this? Well, here is some encouragement. God gives us all desires. Temptation is what Satan uses to get us to give into our desires in the wrong way. The enemy uses bait to lure us into disobedience, but God has given us the gift of the fruit of the Spirit. Part of this gift is self control, and it is the Holy Spirit that helps us exercise and grow in it. We must pray for help, and remember that Satan may tempt us with "bargains", but God always gives gifts and His gifts are always better.

Prayer:

Abba, You have lavished my life with so many wonderful gifts. Through Your loving mercy and grace, I get to live eternally with You through Jesus Christ. I also have the great gift of Your Holy Spirit, my guarantee and seal that I will never be separated from You. Part of this glorious gift also includes sweet and satisfying fruit that gives peace to my spirit, sets my soul on holy fire, and brings my thoughts under Christ's obedience. Self-control is an area that I sometimes find difficulty in. Whether it is through the company I keep, the food I eat, the words I use, or other things that my flesh vies to take the lead on, I know that I get to choose the direction to follow. May I be sensitive to Your Holy Spirit, and always choose Your path. I lay my life down before you, and pray that You rid me of anything that is a hindrance to my spiritual growth and relationship with You. Lead me, Holy Spirit. In Christ's name I pray. Amen.

DAY THIRTY-THREE

Be Encouraged! Listen closely with a...

Jesus Filter

"Understand this, dear brothers and sisters: You must all be quick to listen, slow to speak, and slow to get angry...But don't just listen to God's word. You must do what it says. Otherwise, you are only fooling yourselves." ~James 1:19, 22

As people, we struggle so much with listening to one another. It is like we listen through some kind of self-devised filter; and instead of hearing what someone actually says, we hear what we think it "sounds" like. Our own views, hurts, experiences, and degree of understanding sometimes become an obstacle, and our ears are fixed to position our words with opposition and judgment. I find this interesting, especially within the Church. I think about all the missed opportunities to hear the heart of another. I think about how we miss opportunities to practice loving whole-heartedly in EVERY situation. I wonder what it would look like if we just listened with a Jesus filter. I mean, what if we just listened to one another without looking for error. Communication does not have to be as difficult as we make it, neither does embracing someone else despite indifference. Go forth, and listen with godly love!

Prayer:

Lord, since the beginning of creation, You have shown us through Your great love how to be in relationship with others and how to communicate in love. Communication begins with us first learning how to listen. This is why You have commanded us to be quick to listen and slow to speak. May I follow the example of Christ in listening to the heart of another, and trusting the discernment and guidance of Your Holy Spirit to know how I should respond. Whether the response is an encouraging word, a hug, extra grace in silence, cheer, or shared tears, may it always be done with godly love. May Your glorious filter remove any selfish and unedifying thing in me, as I love as I am called to. Consume my heart, Lord. In Christ's name I pray. Amen.

DAY THIRTY-FOUR

Be Encouraged! Know that your...

Words Matter

"Sometimes it praises our Lord and Father, and sometimes it curses those who have been in the image of God. And so blessing and cursing come pouring out of the same mouth. Surely, my brothers and sisters, this is not right!

~James 3:9-10

I grew up hearing, "sticks and stones may break my bones, but words will never hurt me." This is a great untruth. In the Book of James 3:1-12 we are reminded that words *are* powerful. We get to choose whether we build someone up, or tear them down. As a Christ follower, the words we speak will definitely reveal what is in our hearts. Let our words radiate the love of Christ because words really do matter. Love and Hugs.

Prayer:

Lord, You have created me to be love, for I am made in Your great and magnificent image. This means that the love You pour into me is the same love that I should be pouring into the lives of others. Through Christ I am no longer subject to condemnation, and I have no place to put that burden of guilt or shame on anyone else. May I remember this as I choose the words that reveal my true heart. May I always speak life and love. May my words reflect the choice that I have made to follow You all the days of my life. In Jesus Christ's name I pray. Amen.

DAY THIRTY-FIVE

Be Encouraged! Be strong in setting...

Healthy Boundaries

"Share each other's burdens, and in this way obey the law of Christ...Pay careful attention to your own work, for then you will get the satisfaction of a job well done, and you won't need to compare yourself to anyone else. For we are each responsible for our own conduct."

~Galatians 6:2, 4-5

Boundaries are necessary for healthy relationships. It is okay to say no. It is okay that some people will not like you setting boundaries. It is not our job to take on everybody else's responsibility. It is not our job to deal with the repercussions of someone else's choices (Galatians 6:5). It is our job, however, to love others (Galatians 6:2). Loving others sometimes means saying no, putting our foot down, and getting out of the way of the One that can help them most. We can only do what God has given us responsibility to do...that's it! When we try going above that, we will most assuredly find stress. We do a serious disservice to others when we get in the way of their own growth process by enabling them. So setting and keeping boundaries is a great way to foster healthy relationships, encourage the growth of others, and teach people the way you wish to be treated.

Prayer:
Lord, I pray that You would direct my steps and my intention in how I learn how to have healthy relationships. You teach me in Your Word that even though I am responsible to others, I am not responsible for others. Forgive me for the times when I have gone outside the boundary You have set for me. May I walk in the understanding that You alone are Savior to all. I pray that the love, support, and encouragement I pour into others reflect the love and obedience I have been called to. Let me no longer be a hindrance to the spiritual growth of anyone I encounter in my journey. Instead, may I love in Your wisdom and grace as a pleasing fragrance to You and those You have called me to serve. All for Your glory! In Jesus Christ's name I pray. Amen.

DAY THIRTY-SIX

Be Encouraged! Be still and...

Listen Up

"He will most certainly be gracious to you at the sound of your cry for help; when He hears it, He will answer you. Though the Lord gives you the bread of adversity and the water of oppression, yet your Teacher will no longer hide Himself, but your eyes will [constantly] see your Teacher. Your ears will hear a word behind you, "This is the way, walk in it", whenever you turn to the right or to the left."

~Isaiah 30:19b-21, AMP

No one hears from God in the same way. He is limitless in how He communicates with us. It can be through His Word, prayer, another person, a situation, nature, etc. For some, it is a still small voice, for others it is a definite stirring in their heart. There are just so many ways. If we sit waiting on some kind of "show", we can miss out on really connecting with Him. He is literally everywhere. We have to learn to be quiet enough to hear Him. The distractions of life tend to get in the way. We let so much get in the way, but God promises throughout His Word that when we call, He will answer. Do we believe that? Do we believe it enough to do it? What would happen if we just asked God to speak to us, and then just sat there quietly, patiently waiting to hear from Him?

Prayer:

Father, with surrendered heart I pray that You are my sole's only devotion. May my focus and affection be lifted up to You with my arms wide open in humble love. I truly am Yours, and You promise that You will always be with me. You promise that You will always give me the way to walk in. How amazing is Your love for me, Lord! That You would bless me richly with such great Counsel through Your Holy Spirit. May Your all surpassing peace, love, and grace drown out all that tries to distract me from You. May I sit at Your feet and listen to Your gentle whispers that fill my heart. May I forever be reminded that when I call upon Your name, You will always answer, and it will always be for my good. My life for Your glory, in Jesus Christ's name. Amen.

DAY THIRTY-SEVEN

Be Encouraged! Rejoice in your...

Blessings in the Moment

"Not that I was ever in need, for I have learned how to be content with whatever I have. I know how to live on almost nothing or with everything. I have learned the secret of living in every situation, whether it is full stomach or empty, with plenty or little. For I can do everything through Christ, who gives me strength."

~Philippians 4:11-13

As Christ followers, we should have a firm belief in knowing and trusting that God has a plethora of blessings for us throughout our lives. However, it is easy for us to focus only on that next blessing. Not to dismiss or devalue "yet blessings" and "yet to comes", but it should be urged for us as God's children to make sure we see the blessings in today. If we only look at what we want and pray for God to do next, then we totally miss out on what He has done and given us in the now. Being content is not the same as being complacent; and content is okay. Content helps us to be grateful in our now, ask Paul (check out Philippians 4). Just remember, God's love for us is unconditionally good in all times: past, present, and future. Start celebrating where He has brought you from, where He has you now, and where He will bring you yet to come. Live in joy!

Prayer:

Father God, You are the greatest Provider in my life. There is not one part of who I am and the journey that I am on where You have not poured Your hand of blessing upon me. Thank You for being so gracious to me. I know that I can sometimes get wrapped up in my long list of wants, and that can be a distraction from me seeing all the goodness of Your presence and presents around me. Forgive me for being so self-absorbed. I pray that Your Holy Spirit help me to walk in humility, with open eyes, and full heart to Your wonder. May my prayers be rich with thanksgiving, praises, and awe to Your glory and loving nature. You are the best Father ever, and I am thankful that nothing will ever separate me from my truth in Your promise. In Jesus Christ's name I pray. Amen!

DAY THIRTY-EIGHT

Be Encouraged! Set your heart on...

Better Expectations

"Heed the sound of my cry for help, my King and my God, for to You I pray. In the morning I will prepare [a prayer and sacrifice] for You and watch and wait [for You to speak to my heart]."

~Psalms 5:2-3, AMP

When we read the Bible, every time we find the words expect or expectation, it references God. Every expectation we are taught to have as Christ followers, is solely in what God can and will do. So why do we have them for ourselves and others? Outside of God, expectations are really just a disappointment waiting to happen. That is a lot to place on anyone who was never supposed to bear the weight of such responsibility. We can *hope* that someone keeps to the things they are responsible for. We can *hope* that we meet the goals and dreams we wish to accomplish, but we can only expect God's will to prevail every step of the way. We just do not have the authority to place that kind of authority on someone else. So instead of focusing on misplaced expectations, focus on God and expect Him to provide in ways you could not imagine or ask.

Prayer:

Lord, let me not be conformed to the ways of this world regarding expectations. The only confidence that is beneficial to my soul is confidence in You. Help me to no longer place unhealthy expectations on myself or those around me. Help me to be expectant only in what You will do. May I be bold in my prayers to You, and strong in my patience to see what Your perfect will is for me. May I exchange holding unhealthy expectations for increased hope. Hope in You is never burdensome, will never fail, and I will always keep my focus where it should be: "On an everlasting Father who literally has given me the moon and stars simply because He loves me". Thank You, Lord. I am forever grateful and humble in Your presence. In Jesus Christ's name I praise You always. Amen.

DAY THIRTY-NINE

Be Encouraged! Let your words speak...

Blessings over Everything

"And don't grumble as some of them did, and then were destroyed by the angel of death. These things happened to them as examples for us. They were written down to warn us who live at the end of age."
~1 Corinthians 10:10-11

I have a confession to make. Sometimes I struggle with being quick to complain and grumble about my flaws and unmet expectations. As unintentional as it may happen, it is very dangerous to my spirit. I am not sure if you share in the same struggle, but I want to speak to the heart of those that do.

Scripture teaches that complaining is a spirit killer. At the core of who we are, we find God and His great love. Giving in to the negativity and lies by speaking outside of our truth, is essentially giving in to Satan's tactics. Sure it is easy to see where we do not fit into the world's standards, but that is okay since we were never created to fit in the first place. Life happens, but we must not recognize burdens before blessings. It is essential to adjust our vision so we see the hand of God first in everything. It is choosing to be moved by the Holy Spirit, instead of unhealthy thinking and disappointing circumstances. So, let us begin today by focusing what is positive and true. Remember, you were made in the image of Greatness, and the blessings in your life will always far exceed anything you encounter. Just look a little closer, and you will see what God has been doing. Love and hugs!

Prayer:

Lord, forgive me for not always seeing my life through a godly lens. Although I live in a world where it is easy to fixate on the things that are not right, Lord, help me to remember that my truth in You rests in righteousness and all that is good. May my lips be full of praises, and void of complaints. May I see the many blessings in my life, and no longer be blinded by the unhealthy expectations and limitations of this world. You are my joy, Father God, the Giver of life to my spirit, and the center of all that I am. Thank You, for the promises and covering I receive from You daily. In Jesus Christ's name I pray. Amen.

DAY FORTY

Be Encouraged! Your path is clear with...

God-Given Vision

"This vision is for a future time. It describes the end, and it will be fulfilled. If it seems slow in coming, wait patiently, for it will surely take place. It will not be delayed."
~Habakkuk 2:3

Vision is a beautiful thing. It is one of those gifts from God that transcends deeper than a physical attribute. Vision adds fire to the embers of our purpose and calling in life. It excites our spirit, and motivates passions that God placed intricately within us as we were formed. Every person has a God-given vision assigned to their life. Sometimes, however, every day distractions and obstacles either keep us blinded or blurred to what we see. Sometimes, in our own impatience, we rush through the value of moments leading to the vision.

In both instances it is important to remember that when God gives us these visions, there is life-giving spiritual growth found in every step towards reaching that goal. We cannot be lax about it, just as we cannot be too eager. There is balance and a steady pace to seeing the vision God blesses us with that can only be found through the Holy Spirit's guidance. It means that we have to trust God's perfect plan and time through the entire process of Him planting, cultivating, pruning, weeding, and harvesting this gift. It means being obedient, and surrendering ourselves wholly to His agenda. This adds new meaning to seeing life through a godly lens. Let the eyes of your spirit see the clear path God is making for you, and may your heart and feet be quickened to follow Him without doubt or overzealous haste. Your God-given vision is just for you, and the Lord will always follow through on what He has purposed. Take time to truly enjoy every moment in your beautiful journey.

Prayer:
Lord, please help me to not be anxious regarding the vision You have given me. Help me to be patient in lieu of my eager anticipation. As my heart dances with joy seeing Your goodness unfold in my life, I pray that I savor every moment versus rushing to the next. Thank You for the fire You have placed down in my soul. Let these flames of life within me dance to the beat of Your great Sovereignty, Lord. May I never stop wanting more of You. In Your wonderful Son's name, Jesus Christ, I pray, Amen.

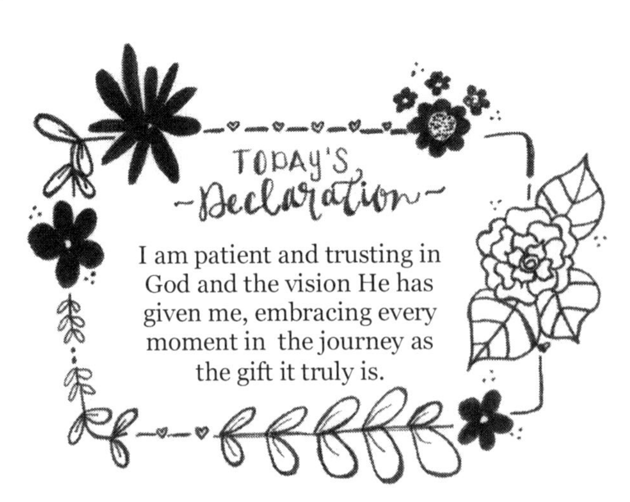

CONGRATULATIONS!

You completed your 40 day journey of encouragement and prayer. The next step is to remember these loving truths about who you are, and to trust where God is directing you in your life. Your story serves a great purpose in a much more amazing and divine design. I pray that you never short yourself of the beauty that dwells within you. Walk with your head held high knowing that you are a child of a Great and Sovereign Father, and the radiant colors of your spirit add so much to a dim and dying world. Now...

Say this out loud:
I am AMAZING!
I am EXTRAORDINARY!
I have GREAT VALUE!
I am LOVED!
I am A CHERISHED CHILD OF THE MOST HIGH GOD!

Now, go live your day knowing that you have spoken a truth that God has already declared over your life. Oh, and while we are at it, here is one more prayer and declaration to begin the next part of your journey. Be blessed!

Prayer:

Thank You, Abba, that who I am is rooted in You. No one knows me better than You, and by Your love I am called a masterpiece. May You strike down every lie that tries to set itself against me as Your beloved child, and co-heir with the One True King, Jesus Christ. May I never seek to be filled by anything other than the One who satisfies deeper than I can fathom. Lord, may I walk with godly truth in my step, and the sweet song of Your good news on my lips. Help me to see beyond the façade that this world has to offer, and embrace Your gifts of freedom, acceptance, security, purpose, and value through Christ. My heart is forever Yours, for You alone truly do complete me. May Your wonderful glory and kingdom come, may You be my praise always. In Jesus Christ's name I pray. Amen!

NOTES

NOTES

NOTES

NOTES

NOTES

THE LORD SAYS,

I will GUIDE YOU along the BEST pathway FOR your life. I WILL advise you AND WATCH over YOU.

PSALMS 32:8

dk

Made in the USA
Columbia, SC
02 October 2017